YOUR OXYGEN MASK FIRST WORKBOOK

17 Habits to Help High Achievers Survive & Thrive

in Leadership & Life

ISBN   978-1-5445-1024-8

LIONCREST
PUBLISHING

17 HABITS TO HELP HIGH ACHIEVERS SURVIVE & THRIVE IN LEADERSHIP & LIFE

YOUR
OXYGEN MASK
FIRST
WORKBOOK

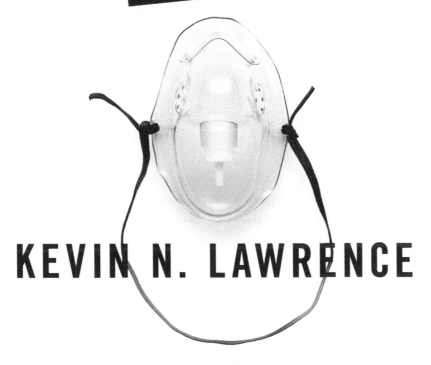

KEVIN N. LAWRENCE

CONTENTS

Chapter 1. Live an Amazing Life   9

Chapter 2. Forget Work-Life Balance   14

Chapter 3. Double Your Resilience   15

Chapter 4. Invest In Your Sweet Spots   25

Chapter 5. Lick Your Toads   31

Chapter 6. Deal With Your Emotional Junk   37

Chapter 7. Manage Your Mental Health   41

Chapter 8. Learn Like Your Life Depends on It   47

Chapter 9. Get Tough Feedback   51

Chapter 10. Make Yourself Useless   57

Chapter 11. Quadruple Your IQ   65

Chapter 12. Stop Being Chief Problem Solver   71

Chapter 13. Teach People to Meet Your Standards   75

Chapter 14. Tackle Tough Conversations   79

Chapter 15. Love the Lessons   83

Chapter 16. Keep Going For It   89

Chapter 17. Plan, Plan and Plan Again   93

Parting Words   101

Additional Resources from Coach Kevin   103

Appendix — Self Assessment   105

About Coach Kevin   109

For detailed instructions on how to complete these exercises,
please reference the book or audiobook
***Your Oxygen Mask First: 17 Habits to Help High Achievers Survive
& Thrive in Leadership & Life***.

More information at *Lawrenceandco.com*

1

LIVE AN AMAZING LIFE

If you don't make time to enjoy what you

achieve, your life might look great,

but it won't feel great.

"Life is a great big canvas, and you should

throw all the paint on it you can."

DANNY KAYE, actor

Six Steps to Mastery

1. Figure out what makes your life amazing so far

Memories of your life's highlights are a sure-fire way to cut through the head success, and find out what heart success really is to you.

Action

Fill out the 1st column of Amazing Memories Grid.

THE AMAZING MEMORIES GRID

AMAZING MEMORY	HEAD SUCCESS (ACHIEVEMENT) & WHY	HEART SUCCESS (ENJOYMENT) & WHY
1.		
2.		
3.		
4.		
5.		

2. Notice which successes mean the most

Fill out the 2nd and 3rd columns on the Amazing Memories Grid. For each amazing memory note if it gave you a deep sense of enjoyment (heart success) or a sense of achievement (head success) – or both. Note why.

3. Discover what you would do if you had complete choice and freedom

Action

You receive news that a long-lost relative has left you a $50 million inheritance, but you have to work at least 30 hours a week, and your enjoyment of work, and life must average at least eight out of 10:

- What activities and pursuits would you start doing (or do more often)?
- What activities and pursuits would you stop doing (or do less often)?

Fill out the 1st row on the Amazing Life Grid.

AMAZING LIFE GRID

	START DOING (OR DO MORE) & WHY	STOP DOING (OR DO LESS) & WHY
$50 MILLION INHERITANCE		
12-YEAR-OLD WISDOM		
82-YEAR-OLD WISDOM		
GAME-OVER WISDOM		

4. Get advice from Young You, Old You and Game-Over You

a. 12-Year-Old Wisdom: Imagine describing your life so far to a 12-year old version of yourself.

Action

What changes would that child want you to make right now? Fill out the 2nd row on the Amazing Life Grid.

b. 82-Year-Old Wisdom: Imagine describing your life so far to an 82-year old version of yourself.

Action

What changes would that 82-year old want you to make right now? Fill out the 3rd row on the Amazing Life Grid.

c. Game-Over Wisdom: Nothing is quite as clarifying as mortality.

Action

If you knew this is your final year on this great planet, how would you spend your days? What would you stop doing? Fill out the 4th row on the Amazing Life Grid.

5. Put it all together: Your Amazing Life Plan

Take what you've learned from the previous exercises. What themes or patterns do you notice?

_____

_____

_____

_____

_____

Action

Based on what you learned from the previous exercises, fill out the Amazing Life Plan Grid. Choose your top three 'achievement' _and_ top three 'enjoyment' goals for the next 12 months.

Tip

Start with the 'Self' category.

AMAZING LIFE PLAN GRID

	ACHIEVEMENT	ENJOYMENT
WORK		
SELF		
LIFE		

6. Build a better plan, and plan ahead – well ahead

Tip
Use birthdays and holidays to your advantage. These are great triggers for scheduling special events and get-togethers.

Action
What key things do you need to schedule for the coming 12 to 18 months?

1.
2.
3.
4.
5.

Tip
Think of your life as a massive R&D project. Keep experimenting, notice what works and what doesn't, and adjust at you go. An amazing life is an evolving life.

Gut Check
Be brutally honest – how good are you at *enjoying life* in tandem with your achievements in business?
On a scale of 0 (low) to 10 (high): _____

Simple Summary

Success isn't *only* what you achieve or possess. It's how you *feel* about your life.

2

FORGET WORK-LIFE BALANCE

Dump the notion of work-life balance.

Focus on work-self-life passion instead.

"You don't go to the amusement park roller coaster and say, 'I want to be balanced'. No, you want to be as unbalanced as possible, because that's the thrill of the ride."

NEIL DEGRASSE TYSON, astrophysicist

Four Steps to Mastery

1. Do a reality check: Passion Ratios

Action
Look back over the past month. What percentage of your best energy and creativity did you use for work, self and life? Fill out the first row of the Passion Ratio Grid.

2. Pick your ideal split
Choose your ideal Passion Ratio. Start with the 'self' category, or you may find only a small percentage of passion left for you. Fill out the second row of the Passion Ratio Grid.

3. Choose differently
What do you need to start—or stop—doing to align to your Ideal Passion Ratio? Fill out the Passion Ratio Grid.

PASSION RATIO GRID

	WORK	SELF	LIFE
CURRENT PASSION RATIO	_____ %	_____ %	_____ %
IDEAL PASSION RATIO	_____ %	_____ %	_____ %
START OR DO MORE OFTEN			
STOP OR DO LESS OFTEN			

4. Keep tweaking

Make sure you reflect on your Passion Ratio every time you do your annual and quarterly planning. Always do this in writing, noting your observations, and the tweaks that need to happen.

Gut Check

Do you dedicate enough time and energy for everything that matters:

your work, self & life?

On a scale of 0 (low) to 10 (high): _____

Simple Summary

Invest passion units in yourself first, to be as giving and productive as you want to be in other aspects of your life.

3

DOUBLE YOUR RESILIENCE

When you stay true to your Resilience Rituals, you set yourself up to win, no matter what life throws at you.

"A good half of the art of living is resilience."

ALAIN DE BOTTON, Swiss-born British author

Five Steps to Mastery

1. Know your history

Think about the periods in your life when you felt fantastic and amazingly strong. I don't mean individual moments – I mean ongoing periods of time when you felt inspired, buoyant and invincible. What were you doing to take care of your body, mind and spirit?

Action

Fill out the When I Felt Strongest Grid thinking about three different times you were at your best.

WHEN I FELT STRONGEST GRID

TIME PERIOD	1.	2.	3.
BODY: HOW DID I KEEP MY BODY FEELING ENERGIZED AND/OR STRONG?			
MIND: HOW DID I KEEP MY MIND CLEAR AND/OR FOCUSED?			
SPIRIT: WHAT DID I FIND REWARDING AND/OR INSPIRING?			

2. Deepen your understanding

All three aspects of your Resilience Rituals (body, mind and spirit) are mission critical and interdependent. It's crucial to understand the importance of each one.

Action

Fill out the Resilience Ritual Brainstorming Grid.

RESILIENCE RITUAL BRAINSTORMING GRID

BODY: WHAT MAKES YOU FEEL PHYSICALLY AT YOUR BEST?	
MIND: WHAT HELPS YOU CLEAR YOUR HEAD AND GET FOCUSED?	
SPIRIT: WHAT ACTIVITIES LIGHT YOU UP INSIDE?	

3. Draft your Resilience Rituals

Reflect on what you wrote in exercises #1 and #2, as well as anything else you know about what makes you feel strong and vibrant. Based on your insights, create a first draft of your Resilience Rituals.

Action

Fill out the first two columns (What & Frequency) on the My Resilience Rituals Grid.

MY RESILIENCE RITUALS GRID

	WHAT	FREQUENCY	WHEN
BODY	• •		
MIND	• •		
SPIRIT	• •		

KEVIN'S RESILIENCE RITUALS GRID

	WHAT	FREQUENCY	WHEN
BODY	• Workout with trainer • Other activities: Walk, bike or hike	3× a week 3× a week	6am 6am or on weekends
MIND	• Journal for 10 -15 minutes • Update my to-do lists	3× a week 5× a week	7am (after workout) 8:00am (weekdays)
SPIRIT	• Adventures with loved ones • Push my limits with like-minded people (e.g. motorsports)	2× a month 1 to 2× a month	Weekends, evenings Weekends

4. Commit to your Resilience Rituals – even when they anger or annoy others

When will you do each of your Resilience Rituals activities? Fill in the 'When' category on the Resilience Rituals Grid.

5. Adjust your Resilience Rituals as needed

Keep looking for other ways to improve your Resilience Rituals. Test to see if you notice an improvement or not.

Gut Check

How good are you at making time for things that build and maintain your personal resilience: body, mind and spirit? On a scale of 0 (low) to 10 (high): _____

Simple Summary

When your strength and resilience are a priority, you'll have the stamina to give even more.

4

INVEST IN YOUR SWEET SPOTS

Spend 80% of your time and energy doing things

you love to do, the way you love to do them.

"Success is achieved by developing our
strengths, not by eliminating our weaknesses."

MARILYN VON SAVANT,
highest recorded IQ in the "Guinness Book of Records"

Six Steps to Mastery

1. Examine your patterns of success to understand your natural ability

Success leaves clues. Your sweet spot is similar throughout your life. The reason you were class valedictorian, or a track star, is probably similar to the reason your first company was a smashing success.

Action

Take a look at your track record, and fill out the first two columns on the Historical Sweet Spots Grid. Make a list of your top five achievements to date, in work and life. For each one, note what natural ability made you succeed.

HISTORICAL SWEET SPOTS GRID

ACHIEVEMENT	NATURAL ABILITY	ENVIRONMENT
1.		
2.		
3.		
4.		
5.		

2. Know your ideal environment

Pinpoint the environmental factors that matter to you by looking again at your top five achievements on the Historical Sweet Spots Grid. Fill out the 3rd column, noting the defining features of the environment.

Some things to consider:

- Was it a team environment or an individual situation?
- If it was a team, was it a new team or one with a long history?
- Were you under a lot of pressure or not?
- Was there an urgent deadline or not?
- Was there a creative aspect to your role?
- Did you create something brand new, or improve something that already existed?
- Was it a global project? Local?

3. Notice what you love about your work (past and present)

Fill out the 'Love To Do' list.

LOVE TO DO LIST

WHAT ENERGIZES ME WHAT I LOVE TO DO	WHAT DRAINS ME WHAT I AVOID

4. Draft Your Sweet Spot

Articulate your sweet spot.

My Sweet Spot

What I love to do, and do well:

_____

_____

_____

_____

How I love to do it (i.e. the environment):

_____

_____

_____

_____

5. Move toward spending 80% of your time in your sweet spot

Do an honest assessment of your current situation. How much time do you currently spend in your sweet spot, doing work you love, and how you love doing it?

Sweet Spot Reality Check

Current % of time: _____%

Goal for next six months: _____%

6. Making the shift

How will you move more toward spending 80% of your time in your sweet spot? List three things you need to start doing (or do more often), and three things you need to stop doing (or do less often).

What do I need to start doing (or do more often)?

1.	
2.	
3.	

What do I need to stop doing (or do less often)?

1.	
2.	
3.	

Tip

Self-assessments can really help you zero in on your sweet spot. They give you a model for understanding your natural strengths. My favourites are *DiSC* and *Strengths*. Both are reasonably inexpensive, quick and painless, and give valuable insight you can apply immediately.

Gut Check

How good are you at spending the vast majority of your time and energy doing things you love and are good at?

On a scale of 0 (low) to 10 (high): _____

Simple Summary

Stop boring yourself or torturing yourself with tasks outside your sweet spot.
You deliver the most value doing what you love.

5

LICK YOUR TOADS

Get your toads done so your energy is freed up for

bigger and better things.

"You may delay, but time will not."

BENJAMIN FRANKLIN

25 Common Toads

1. Giving feedback to underperforming employees
2. Changing roles for employees
3. Firing or demoting employees
4. Saying no
5. Dealing with unresolved conflicts
6. Asking customers for feedback
7. Calling customers for money
8. Firing bad clients
9. Thanking customers
10. Telling a client you made a mistake
11. Tolerating late or incorrect orders
12. Closing or selling a business, or part of a business
13. Ending or renegotiating a joint venture
14. Booking vacations and taking time to recharge
15. Scheduling doctors appointments
16. Spending quality time with loved ones
17. Making decisions related to family, home and finances
18. Unresolved conflicts or arguments
19. Finding a therapist
20. Planning for retirement
21. Doing your taxes
22. Doing your will
23. Dealing with clutter at home
24. Handling home repairs
25. Working on personal relationships.

Five Steps to Mastery

1. Know your toads

Unlock the toads from the recesses of your mind. Dig 'em out.

Write 'em down. Make a list of every single one, large and small.

Include every to-do that gives you an unpleasant twinge when it pops into your head. Just getting these down on paper is an achievement, because it will spur you to take action.

Action

Write down the first 30 toads that come to your mind. Use the '25 Common Toads' list as a prompt.

30 TOADS

1.	
2.	
3.	
4.	
5.	
6.	
7.	
8.	
9.	
10.	
11.	
12.	
13.	
14.	
15.	
16.	
17.	
18.	
19.	
20.	
21.	
22.	
23.	
24.	
25.	
26.	
27.	
28.	
29.	
30.	

2. Lick 10 toads in 10 days

Pick 10 toads from your 30 Toads list to complete within a 10-day period. Write them in the 1ˢᵗ column of the My First 10 Toads Grid.

Tip

You might like to pick easy toads to kick-start some momentum. Or you might want to tackle some tough ones that really drag you down. Or a combo. Do what motivates you most.

MY FIRST 10 TOADS GRID

TOAD	THE "D" TO USE
1.	
2.	
3	
4.	
5.	
6.	
7.	
8.	
9.	
10.	

3. Employ the Five D's

There's more than one way to lick a toad. It's not always appropriate for you to personally handle it. Sometimes it's not yours to do at all. Sometimes you know it'll never happen if it stays in your court.

1. **Do it.** Bite the bullet immediately.

2. **Don't do it**. Say 'no' to the person who requested it, if it's simply not yours to do.

3. **Delegate it**. Assign an appropriate person.

4. **Delete it**. Let go of it entirely. Decide it's not going to happen.

5. **Date it**. Commit to completing it by a specific date sometime down the road. _Do not_ use this as a default. Only apply this when now is truly not the right time to deal with the task.

Action

Refer back to the My First 10 Toads Grid. For each toad, note which of the Five D's you will use.

6. Lick your nastiest toad first thing every morning

Make a top three list to complete before you start your day tomorrow.

TODAY'S TOP THREE TOADS

1.
2.
3.

7. Schedule a Toad Day at the office

Pick a potential date for your first team Toad Day.

_____

Tip

You can call Toad Day whatever you want, of course – Spring Cleaning Day, Fresh Start Day, Catch Up Day. Whatever fits your corporate culture.

Gut Check

How do you rate at making sure annoying little things get done before they pile up?
On a scale of 0 (low) to 10 (high): _____

Simple Summary

The little things you procrastinate consume far more energy than you believe.
Get them out of the way.

6

DEAL WITH YOUR EMOTIONAL JUNK

Get rid of your emotional junk so that it doesn't cause bad decisions or regrettable behaviour.

"We are enslaved by anything we do not consciously see. We are freed by conscious perception."

VERNON HOWARD, author, spiritual teacher, philosopher

Five Steps to Mastery

1. If you're emotional, don't decide or react

Next time you're feeling emotional about a decision, or something you're about to do, wait 24 hours, and let the emotion subside.

2. Know your emotional junk

Use the Emotional Junk Grid to track what causes your bad decisions, or regrettable behaviour.

Action

Fill out the first two columns of the Emotional Junk Grid.

EMOTIONAL JUNK GRID EXAMPLE

BAD DECISION OR REGRETTABLE BEHAVIOUR	EMOTIONAL JUNK	WORKAROUND
1. Waited to fire employee	Uncomfortable with conflict	Get HR involved early
2. Hired the wrong ad agency	Pressured by marketing VP	Express opinion in writing when pressured
3. Unsafe driving to meeting	Worry clients will lose respect	Leave 15 minutes earlier than you think you need to
4. Yelled at employee	Triggered by disrespect	End conversations as soon as anger arises

EMOTIONAL JUNK GRID

BAD DECISION OR REGRETTABLE BEHAVIOUR	EMOTIONAL JUNK	WORKAROUND
1.		
2.		
3.		
4.		

3. Have workarounds

Fill out the 'Workaround' column on the Emotional Junk Grid.

4. Know the warning signs

What physical or emotional sensations are warning signs that you're getting triggered to behave badly, or make a regrettable decision?

WARNING SIGN	WHAT'S ABOUT TO HAPPEN
1.	
2.	
3.	
4.	
5.	

5. Clean up the junk

Which professional(s) could help you clean up your emotional junk? Contact one this week to get the ball rolling.

1.	
2.	

Gut Check

How good are you at *not* responding irrationally or emotionally in tense situations? On a scale of 0 (low) to 10 (high): _____

Simple Summary

Don't let emotional junk hold you back as a leader.

7

MANAGE YOUR
MENTAL HEALTH

Have a plan and a back-up plan

for managing your mind.

"It's not the heavy load that breaks you down.

It's the way you carry it."

LENA HORNE, jazz icon & civil rights activist

Six Steps to Mastery

1. Notice when stress starts to crack your armour

MENTAL HEALTH CONTINUUM MODEL

HEALTHY	REACTING	INJURED	ILL
Normal mood fluctuations	Irritable/impatient	Angry	Angry outbursts / Aggression
Calm & takes things in stride	Nervous	Anxious	Excessive anxiety / Panic attacks
Good sense of humor	Sad / Overwhelmed	Pervasively sad / Hopeless	Depressed / Suicidal thoughts
Performing well	Displaced sarcasm	Negative attitude	Over insubordination
In control mentally	Procrastination / Forgetfulness	Poor performance / Workaholic Poor concentration & decision-making	Can't perform duties, control behavior, or concentrate
Normal sleep patterns Few sleep difficulties	Trouble sleeping Intrusive thoughts / Nightmares	Restless disturbed sleep Recurrent images / Nightmares	Can't fall asleep or stay asleep / Sleeping too much or too little
Physically well	Muscle tension / Headaches	Increased aches and pains	Physical illnesses
Good energy level	Low energy	Increased fatigue	Constant fatigue
Physically and socially active	Decreased activity and socializing	Avoidance / Withdrawal	Not going out or answering phone
No or limited alcohol use / Gambling	Regular but controlled alcohol use / Gambling	Increased alcohol use / Gambling is hard to control	Alcohol or gambling addiction / Other addictions

Action

Review the Mental Health Continuum: What zone are you in right now?

_____

If you are in the green or yellow zone, make a list of things you can start doing (and/or keep doing), and stop doing (or do less) to strengthen your mental health. *Refer to your Resilience Rituals from Chapter 3* – these are the activities to start doing or do more often.

START (OR DO MORE OFTEN)

1.
2.
3.
4.
5.

STOP (OR DO LESS OFTEN)

1.
2.
3.
4.
5.

If you are in the red or orange zone, make an appointment with your family doctor or a mental health expert, to get back on track. There's more information on this in point 4.

2. Be aware of major life events

There are certain life events that can throw even the most resilient person for a loop. Even one can be shattering, but if someone experiences two of these in close proximity, it's a definite reason to be on alert for warning signs on the Mental Health Continuum.

Major Life Events

Any of these events can trigger a mental health issue:

- Job loss
- Loss of a career dream
- Death of a parent or grandparent (even if elderly)
- Miscarriage
- Abuse
- Sickness or injury (even minor ones that affect lifestyle)
- Sickness or injury of a loved one
- Ending a relationship
- Key support person moving away
- Financial loss or crisis
- Major conflict
- Lawsuit
- Significant mistake
- Getting a new boss
- Loss of a pet
- Kids leaving home.

Action

a. If you're facing one or more of these issues, check in with yourself...are you ok?

- If all is well, great. But keep an eye out for anything unusual.

- If all is not well, go to point four of this chapter and seek help.

b. Is anyone in your life facing one or more of these issues right now? How do they seem to be handling it?

- As above, if all is well—awesome. Watch out for anything unusual.

- If all isn't well, read point four and seek help.

3. Do some mental spring cleaning

Review the Major Life Events list. What past events might be troubling you beneath the surface?

MAJOR LIFE EVENT	OPEN OR HEALED?
1.	
2.	
3.	
4.	
5.	

4. Know who to call

Which mental health pros can you call if an issue arises for you, or someone you know?

a. _____

b. _____

If you're not sure, find someone in your network to connect you with an expert. If you are not sure who to ask, your doctor is a safe bet.

5. Take preventative measures

Your Resilience Rituals are a powerful starting point when it comes to prevention. These are the activities that calm and rejuvenate you. They release the pressure valve on stress.

Action

Which preventative measures do you need to start, or do more often?

PREVENTATIVE MEASURE	WHEN/HOW
1.	
2.	
3.	

6. Have coffee talks

Who might need a coffee talk with you this week?

_____

Gut Check

How skilled are you at managing your mental health?
On a scale of 0 (low) to 10 (high): _____

Simple Summary

It's as essential to take care of your mind, as it is your body.

8

LEARN LIKE YOUR
LIFE DEPENDS ON IT

You need to double your capability every three to
five years to deserve the designation of leadership.

*"The man who does not read has no advantage
over the man who cannot read."*

MARK TWAIN

Five Steps to Mastery

1. Take time to learn

Action

1. How many days a year do you currently invest in strategic learning? This may include reading books, researching online, watching videos, consulting experts; and attending webinars, workshops and conferences.

   Current days per year: _____

2. How many days per year do you feel you would need, to be at your best?

   Needed days per year _____

3. What's the gap between 1 and 2? This is the number of days you need to carve out for additional learning.

   Additional days per year _____

2. Pick your areas

I suggest you break your learning plan into two categories:

a. Strategic Initiatives: Consider the top three to five strategic initiatives you are planning, to achieve your biggest long-term business goals.

Action

Use the Strategic Learning Grid to plan your learning initiatives.

STRATEGIC LEARNING GRID

TOP STRATEGIC INITIATIVES FOR NEXT 3-5 YEARS	WHAT WILL YOU MASTER TO SUPPORT THIS?	HOW WOULD YOU LIKE TO LEARN?	WHEN?
1.			
2.			
3.			
4.			
5.			

b. Personal Fascinations: Your mind is at its sharpest, and most creative, when you allow it to explore its wildest fascinations. I enthusiastically encourage you to think beyond obvious areas of study.

Action

Fill in the first column of Personal Fascinations Grid.

PERSONAL FASCINATIONS GRID

PERSONAL FASCINATION	HOW WOULD YOU LIKE TO LEARN?	WHEN?
1.		
2.		
3.		

3. Know your learning style

Fill out the 'How I would like to learn' columns in the Strategic Learning and Personal Fascinations Grids.

4. Fit learning into your life

Fill in the 'when' columns on the Strategic Learning and Personal Fascinations Grids.

Tip

This will sound crazy, but I listen to audiobooks at 50% faster speed using a function in iTunes. I highly recommend this if audio is your thing. It's a major time-saver, and I find the content more engaging at a faster speed. For the same reason, a speed-reading course is a worthwhile consideration.

5. Get a good ROL (Return on Learning)

Action

What three steps will you take to double your ROL (Return on Learning)?

1.
2.
3.

Gut Check

How do you rate as a lifelong learner?
On a scale of 0 (low) to 10 (high): _____

Simple Summary

Knowledge alone is not the point. You need to put what you learn into practice, or you're no further ahead.

9

GET TOUGH FEEDBACK

Get the truth about your performance,

and how you need to improve.

"The biggest single problem in communication is the illusion that it has taken place."

GEORGE BERNARD SHAW

Five Steps to Mastery

1. Find the truth-tellers

Action

Make a list of your current truth-tellers. Note how you will enlist them to give you even more honesty. Next, create a list of potential truth-tellers, and how you will enlist them.

CURRENT TRUTH-TELLERS

NAME	HOW TO GET MORE TRUTH
1.	
2.	
3.	

POTENTIAL TRUTH-TELLERS

NAME	HOW TO ENLIST
1.	
2.	
3.	

2. Handle honesty well

On a scale of 0 to 10, how gracefully do you receive brutal honesty?

_____

If you are less than a 10 (which 99% of us are), what can you do to receive the truth more gracefully?

1.	
2.	
3.	

3. Extract wisdom via project reviews

Keep your process really simple and really structured. Get the group to discuss only three things:

1. What went well
2. What did not go well (where you got stuck or had challenges)
3. What you learned: three things you'll do differently next time.

Action

Which three projects can you conduct a project review on right away? Who should attend, and when will the meeting be?

	PROJECT	WHO	WHEN
1.			
2.			
3.			

4. If you're going to do 360°s, do them right

360° Action Plan

1. Three areas where you said I'm doing well:

1.	
2.	
3.	

2. Three things you said I need to work on:

1.	
2.	
3.	

3. I'm taking immediate action on _____, because

_____

4. Here's how I'm going to do it _____

5. Here's how you can help me grow _____

Action

1. If your last 360° was less than a year ago, look back to ensure you have improved in the needed areas. If not, complete the 360° Action Plan, and start tomorrow.

2. If your last 360° was more than a year ago, schedule one now.

5. Get a Coach

Action

1. If you don't have a coach, get one. If you need assistance, I can probably help you source a good one in your region. Drop me a note at *kevin@lawrenceandco.com*.

2. If you do have a coach, get twice the value from that relationship by picking three things from this book you would like to master.

THREE THINGS TO MASTER WITH MY COACH

1.
2.
3.

Gut Check

How do you rate at getting honest opinions about your performance?
On a scale of 0 (low) to 10 (high): _____

Simple Summary

You can't be your strongest without the brutal truth.

10

MAKE YOURSELF USELESS

Build a team that delivers better results than you,

without you.

"The growth and development of people is the

highest calling of leadership."

HARVEY S. FIRESTONE, founder of Firestone Tire & Rubber Company

Eight Steps to Mastery

1. Pick your date

Choose the exact date you plan to be completely useless to your business.

Action

Set a date that is relatively soon – no more than five years from now. A longer-term date won't inspire you to take meaningful action.

My Useless Date

My team will be so strong that I will be useless by:

_____

2. Honestly evaluate the performance of each team member

Kevin's Performance Rating System

Here's a simple performance rating system to help you get clear on where you are today:

		PERFORMANCE	
		LOW	HIGH
CULTURE FIT	**HIGH**	B	A
	LOW	C	TOXIC A

Action

1. Rate each of your direct reports as an A, Potential A, Toxic A, B, or C.
2. List why for each one.

DIRECT REPORT	RATING	WHY	ACTION
1.			
2.			
3.			
4.			
5.			
6.			
7.			

What percentage of your direct reports are A-players?

Tip

My website is filled with extensive tools and exercises for evaluating your team. Visit *Lawrenceandco.com*.

3. Live by the motto, 'You have to be an A to stay.'

Action

What action can you take for each of your A-players to make sure each one is challenged enough, but not too much? Fill in the A-Player Grid.

A-PLAYER GRID

A-PLAYER	ACTION
1.	
2.	
3.	
4.	
5.	

4. Help your B-Players become A-Players

Action

For each of your B's, identify an action that could help them evolve into an A-player.

B-PLAYER GRID

B-PLAYER	ACTION
1.	
2.	
3.	
4.	
5.	

5. Quit making excuses for your Toxic A's. And stop hoping they will quit

Action

Identify the action for each of your Toxic A's. This is the final warning or date you will terminate their employment.

TOXIC A GRID

TOXIC A	ACTION
1.	
2.	
3.	
4.	
5.	

6. Manage out the C's

Action

For each of your C's, list the action you can take. Either schedule a time to reiterate the company's culture, their role and what it will take for them to be a fit - or, if you've done this already, put the wheels in motion to set them free. Pick a date for their exit.

C-PLAYER GRID

C-PLAYER	ACTION
1.	
2.	
3.	
4.	
5.	

7. Fire compassionately

Kevin's Tips for Compassionate Firing

There is no perfect or painless method for firing someone, but some ways are better than others.

1. **Treat people fairly**. Give warnings along the way to clearly communicate they are not measuring up, and what needs to change. Document everything, and review what others have documented. Make sure everything is above board.

2. **Help people to move on with dignity.** Help them find a job where they have a better shot at being an A-player. Or at least point them in the right direction. In this way, you empower them to move up, not just move on.

3. **Let them lead the story.** You don't need to destroy someone's reputation simply because they aren't a fit for you. Let them craft the story of their departure. Give them the option of saying 'quit' or 'retired' versus 'fired' when possible.

4. **Treat long-time employees generously.** Yes, there are laws about minimum payouts, but pay more when it feels right. Consider rewarding longevity and past glory with more than is legally required.

5. **Move quickly for their sake and yours.** Waiting will only deplete your energy, and prevent forward motion. Odds are the individual in question knows something is amiss, and needs a catalyst for change.

8. Be ruthless about hiring

Four Fundamentals for Ruthless Hiring

1. Use a proven methodology like *Topgrading*, which is a rigorous system of interviewing. It provides a set of simple questions, and a detailed statistical job description, so it's easier to see who is – and isn't – an A-player.

2. Use a personality profiling system (like *DiSC*) to understand your candidates' natural strengths and working styles.

3. Conduct on-the-job assessments before you hire. Get your candidates to show you the work they can do.

4. Talk to past managers going as far back as you can - at least 15-20 years for experienced executives. You can quickly tell from the tone of the conversation if the person was an A, B or C at each organization.

Action

What three changes can you make to your hiring process to double your odds of finding A-players, and weeding out Toxic A's and C's?

1.
2.
3.

Simple Summary

To have any chance at greatness, leaders must have high-performing, low-maintenance teams.

11

QUADRUPLE YOUR IQ

Have a team of 24 amazing experts

literally a text away.

"Surround yourself only with people who are

going to lift you higher."

OPRAH WINFREY

Five Steps to Mastery

1. Find the gaps on your extended team

Action

Start by listing your current advisors in column one on the Expert Scorecard. Notice the areas where you lack experts. These are items for your to-do list.

EXPERT SCORECARD

EXPERTISE	CURRENT EXPERT	FIT (0 TO 10)	14 X'er (0 TO 10)
WORK EXPERTS			
COACH			
ACCOUNTANT			
LAWYER			
HR CONSULTANT			
MENTOR			
BANKER			
LIFE EXPERTS			
PSYCHOLOGIST/COUNSELLOR			
TRUSTED FRIEND			
TRAVEL AGENT			
INTERIOR DESIGNER			
PARTY PLANNER			
TECHNOLOGY/SOFTWARE EXPERT			

EXPERTISE	CURRENT EXPERT	FIT (0 TO 10)	14 X'er (0 TO 10)
LIFE EXPERTS (CONTINUED)			
SELF-CARE EXPERTS			
COACH			
DOCTOR			
PERSONAL TRAINER			
PSYCHOLOGIST			
PHYSIOTHERAPIST			
OTHER EXPERTS			
GREAT LISTENERS			
CREATIVE PROBLEM SOLVERS			

2. Believe fit matters

Action

Fill in the 'Fit' column of the Expert Scorecard, rating your experts on a scale of 0 (very awkward) to 10 (easy to work with, and brilliant things come from conversations).

3. Use 14 X'ers (aka Don't be anybody's guinea pig)

Action

Fill out the 14 X'er column on the Expert Scorecard to rate the genius level of your current advisors on a scale of 0 (novice) to 10 (brilliant 14 X'er).

4. Strengthen your team: add and upgrade

Action

1. In which areas of expertise do you most need to *add* a genius? Circle your top two or three on the Expert Scorecard.

2. Which experts do you most need to *upgrade* because they are a bad fit, or not a 14X'er, and that area of expertise is currently important to you? Circle two or three of these on your Expert Scorecard.

5. Consider an advisory board

Actions

1. Pick a date when you plan to have your first (or next) advisory board meeting.

_____

2. Decide who will attend the first (or next) meeting.

1.	
2.	
3.	
4.	
5.	

3. Pick three people you aspire to have on your advisory board in the future.

1.	
2.	
3.	

Gut Check

How effective are you at leveraging opinions from experts in business, and in life?
On a scale of 0 (low) to 10 (high): _____

Simple Summary

Get yourself a whole bunch of genius on tap, even if you only access it now and again.

12

STOP BEING CHIEF PROBLEM SOLVER

Require your team to make 90%

of decisions on their own.

"Give a man a fish, he eats for a day.

Teach a man to fish, he eats for a lifetime."

CHINESE PROVERB

Four Steps to Mastery

1. Explain the method to your madness

Action

Who currently makes the decisions on your team?

Decisions made by me: _____%

Decisions made by my team: _____%
(together or individually)

2. Believe in the brilliance of your people

Action

1. Who can you challenge to do more thinking on their own?
2. What can you ask them to make recommendations and/or decisions about?

WHO	WHAT
1.	
2.	
3.	

3. Help people to break through the 'I don't knows'

Action

Which team members ask a lot of questions they probably already know the answers to?

1.	
2.	
3.	

4. Require people to present solutions

Action

Which team members should start bringing you their solutions and recommendations?

1.
2.
3.

Gut Check

How skilled are you are at helping people become strong, independent leaders?
On a scale of 0 (low) to 10 (high): _____

Simple Summary

Make people think for themselves, and they'll get better at it.

13

TEACH PEOPLE TO
MEET YOUR STANDARDS

Tell people what you really expect and hold them to

it without apology.

"Have no fear of perfection.
You'll never reach it."

SALVADOR DALI

Five Steps to Mastery

1. State your expectations up front

Action

How do you really want people to work with you? List five things you wish everyone on your team would *always do* - or *never do* - when working with you.

1.	
2.	
3.	
4.	
5.	

2. Practice requesting the little things that matter to you

Action

What things do you tolerate on a regular basis that can be solved with a simple request?

TOLERATION	REQUEST
1.	
2.	
3.	
4.	
5.	

3. Practice graceful disappointment, and never lower your standards

Action

What kinds of situations cause you to lose your cool? Make a point to employ the method of a calm re-request the next time a situation arises.

TOLERATION	RE-REQUEST
1.	
2.	
3.	
4.	
5.	

4. Up the bar and get more specific

Action

What checklists do you need to create so people can help you to be more successful in high-stakes situations?

MY HIGH-STAKES SITUATIONS LIST

SITUATION	NEEDS
1.	
2.	
3.	

5. Know when to fold 'em

Action

Which team members do you need to...
Give one last chance to meet your expectations?

1.
2.
3.

Break ties with, and find an alternative?

1.
2.
3.

Gut Check

How skilled are you at graciously getting people to meet your high standards?
On a scale of 0 (low) to 10 (high): _____

Simple Summary

Great people will find a way to meet your tough standards.

14

TACKLE TOUGH CONVERSATIONS

Get tough conversations done

within 48 hours.

"I prefer an ugly truth to a pretty lie."

SHAKIRA

Five Steps to Mastery

1. Wait a few hours until the emotion settles

Action

Who do you need to have a tough conversation with in the next 48 hours?

_____

2. Schedule the conversation

Action

What step will you take today to initiate a tough conversation?

_____

3. Plan what you're going to say using my Tough Conversation Model

Tough Conversation Plan

To create the plan for the tough conversation you need to have:

PERMISSION: _____

_____

FACTS: _____

_____

FEELINGS: _____

_____

SUGGESTED RESOLUTION:_____

_____

_____

4. No matter what stick to the plan

Stick to the plan. Stick to the plan.

Stick. To. The. Plan.

You will likely find your conversation takes less than a minute (or some similarly brief period of time). People can't dispute the facts, and they can't dispute your feelings.

5. Have an open mind. Assume you are missing some key information

If you show up to peace talks with a gun in your hand, don't complain later when all hell breaks loose.

Gut Check

How skilled are you are at quickly giving tough feedback?
On a scale of 0 (low) to 10 (high): _____

Simple Summary

Get comfortable delivering the uncomfortable truth quickly.

15

LOVE THE LESSONS

Appreciate that painful experiences make you stronger and smarter.

"I never lose. I either win or learn."

NELSON MANDELA

Four Steps to Mastery

1. Notice the upside of pain

Action

By this point in life, you've had many struggles that shape the person you are today. List five of the most painful challenges you've had to overcome so far in life, and how you grew stronger.

PAINFUL CHALLENGE	HOW I GREW STRONGER

2. Get your money's worth

Action

Fill out the Current Challenge Grid with the current challenges that are most frustrating for you.

CURRENT CHALLENGE GRID

CHALLENGE	WOE STORY	WOW STORY
1.		
2.		
3.		

3. Change your story from 'woe' to 'wow' when it matters most

Action

Look at the challenges in the previous section, and list what your current woe story is. Then, what the wow perspective could be.

4. The Venting Template

Situation _____

1. I hate it when...
   - I can't stand...
   - I'm angry that...

2. It hurt me when...
   - I feel sad when...
   - I feel disappointed about...

3. I was afraid that...
   - I feel scared when...
   - I'm afraid that...

4. I'm sorry that...
   - I did not mean to...
   - Please forgive me for...

5. All I ever wanted was...
   - I want you to...
   - What I want for you is...

6. I understand that...
   - I appreciate...
   - I love you because...

7. I forgive you for...
   - I thank you for...
   - I'm better off now because...

Action

What very difficult situation do you most want to change from a 'woe' story to 'wow' story? Use the Venting Template to help make that shift.

Gut Check

How good are you at seeing the benefit in your challenges, at work and in life?

On a scale of 0 (low) to 10 (high): _____

Simple Summary

Develop the skill to stare challenges dead in the eye, and say, 'wow!' instead of 'woe!'

16

KEEP GOING FOR IT

Keep creating opportunities to be a novice learning

from masters.

"We don't stop playing because we grow old;

we grow old because we stop playing."

GEORGE BERNARD SHAW

Four Steps to Mastery

1. Know what worked in the past

Make a list of the challenging times in your life when you pushed yourself hard, stood on new ground, and became more confident. How did you grow from each situation?

CHALLENGE	HOW I GREW
1.	
2.	
3.	
4.	
5.	

2. Create a Stretch List

Action

Fill out the first column on your Stretch List.

STRETCH LIST

I'D LIKE TO...	LOCAL GUIDE
1.	
2.	
3.	
4.	
5.	
6.	
7.	
8.	
9.	
10.	

3. Find local guides

Action

Fill out the 'Local Guide' column on your Stretch List to indicate where you would like a guide.

4. Just take a step forward. It's never too late to start

Action

Which item on your stretch list calls out most for you to just go for it?

_____

Gut Check

How good are you at regularly stretching your personal limits?
On a scale of 0 (low) to 10 (high): _____

Simple Summary

Keep challenging yourself to stay humble and hungry.

17

PLAN, PLAN AND PLAN AGAIN

Have a simple, all-encompassing,

one-page Master Plan for work,

self and life.

"Everyone has a plan 'till they

get punched in the mouth."

MIKE TYSON, prize fighter

Three Steps to Mastery

1. Commit to annual planning

For your annual planning, use the *My Master Plan** worksheet.

ANNUAL REVIEW
HOW DID THE YEAR GO?

YOUR WORK Career, money, and investments	YOUR SELF Being happy, strong, and healthy	YOUR LIFE Friends, family, and community
Your biggest wins or achievements of the year?		
Your biggest challenges, frustrations or disappointments?		
The biggest lessons from your mistakes?		
PASSION RATIO: How did you invest your energy this year?		
___%	___%	___%
What would have been ideal for you to be your best?		
___%	___%	___%
If you could do the year over again, what would you do differently?		

* Digital downloads available at *Lawrenceandco.com/Books*

MY MASTER PLAN
THE THINGS THAT MATTER MOST

GUIDING VALUES	SWEET SPOT To spend 90% of your time in	WON'T DO OR TOLERATE

	YOUR WORK Career, money, and investments	YOUR SELF Being happy, strong, and healthy	YOUR LIFE Friends, family, and community
The Ultimate in Your Lifetime			
To Achieve			
To Enjoy or Experience			
To Be Remembered For			
Twice As Good In 3 Years			
Passion Ratio	__%	__%	__%
#1 Objective			
#2			
Achieve This Year			
Passion Ratio	__%	__%	__%
#1 Goal			
#2			

QUARTER PLAN

PLAN FOR QUARTER ____ OF ____

	YOUR WORK Career, money, and investments	**YOUR SELF** Being happy, strong, and healthy	**YOUR LIFE** Friends, family, and community
Passion Ratio	___%	___%	___%
#1 Project			
Other projects?			
#2			
#3			
Toads #1			
#2			
Habit To Start*			
Stop			
Actions to take this week?			

* Choose 1 of the 17 habits from this book.

2. Re-plan quarterly

Use the *Quarterly Reset** worksheet toward the end of each quarter to:

a.   Review and reflect on your work, self and life results from the previous quarter.

b.   Plan your focus for the coming quarter.

QUARTERLY RESET
REVIEW OF QUARTER _____ OF _____

YOUR WORK Career, money, and investments	YOUR SELF Being happy, strong, and healthy	YOUR LIFE Friends, family, and community
Biggest achievements?		
Biggest challenges or disappointments?		
PASSION RATIO: How much energy did you invest this quarter?		
___%	___%	___%
What would have been ideal for you to be your best?		
___%	___%	___%
What do you need to Start or Stop doing to be on track with your Annual Goals?		

* Digital downloads available at *Lawrenceandco.com/Books*

QUARTER PLAN

PLAN FOR QUARTER ____ OF ____

	YOUR WORK Career, money, and investments	**YOUR SELF** Being happy, strong, and healthy	**YOUR LIFE** Friends, family, and community
Passion Ratio	___%	___%	___%
#1 Project			
Other projects?			
#2			
#3			
Toads #1			
#2			
Habit To Start*			
Stop			
Actions to take this week?			

* Choose 1 of the 17 habits from this book.

Simple Summary

Your achievements will be greater, and you will enjoy life more, if you make proper planning and re-planning an annual and quarterly discipline.

PARTING WORDS

Standing still kills great leaders.

You can't be the same person you were six months ago, and deal with the challenges your business presents today. You need to be a new person, evolving all the time, continually stepping forward to meet your new reality.

In this way, high-growth leadership is like walking up the down escalator. If you don't take the next step, you slide backward. Staying in the same place isn't an option. You can only move ahead or regress.

The intensity of this commitment isn't for everyone, but when it's for you, you know it.

This book is written specifically to guide you on this journey, with the aim that you keep coming back to it over the years, to continue to strengthen yourself, and to build the habits required to be a masterful leader.

I would love to hear the stories of your leadership journey. I invite you to send anecdotes, suggestions, techniques and tools that work for you.

I will end this book with the very same quote I began, with the genuine wish that you live your version of an amazing life:

"Life should not be a journey to the grave with the intention of arriving safely in a pretty and well preserved body, but rather to skid in broadside in a cloud of smoke, thoroughly used up, totally worn out, and loudly proclaiming, "Wow! What a Ride!"

HUNTER S. THOMPSON

ADDITIONAL RESOURCES FROM COACH KEVIN

Visit *Lawrenceandco.com/Books* where you will find tools, insights, videos and other resources related to this book including:

- *The Your Oxygen Mask First Toolkit*
- *The Oxygen Mask Self-Assessment*

Be sure to check back regularly – I'll frequently add more resources.

Coach Kevin's Top Book Recommendations

1. *Art of War*, Sun Tzu

2. *Built to Last*, Jim Collins & Jerry I. Porras

3. *Blue Ocean Strategy*, Kim/Mauborgne

4. *Clarity: Clear Mind, Better Performance, Bigger Results*, Jamie Smart

5. *Confessions of the Pricing Man*, Hermann Simon

6. *Crucial Conversations*, Patterson/Grenny/McMillan/Swiztler

7. *Daily Rituals: How Artists Work*, Mason Currey

8. *Death By Meeting*, Patrick M. Lencioni

9. *Deep Work*, Cal Newport

10. *Execution*, Ram Charan

11. *Getting More*, Stuart Diamond

12. *Good to Great*, Jim Collins

13. *Great by Choice*, Jim Collins

14. *Great Game of Business*, Jack Stack

15. *Hide a Dagger Behind a Smile*, Kaihan Krippendorf

16. *High Output Management*, Andrew S. Grove

17. *How the Mighty Fall*, Jim Collins

18. *How To Win Friends & Influence People*, Dale Carnegie

19. *Influence*, Robert Cialdini

20. *Islands of Profit in a Sea of Red Ink*, Jonathan L.S. Byrnes

21. *Meetings Suck*, Cameron Herald

22. *Multipliers*, Liz Wiseman & Greg McKeown

23. *Now! Discover Your Strengths*, Marcus Buckingham

24. *Radical Candor*, Kim Scott

25. *Rookie Smarts*, Liz Wiseman

26. *Scaling Up*, Verne Harnish

27. *Scrum*, Jeff Sutherland/JJ Sutherland

28. *Start with Why*, Simon Sinek

29. *Team of Teams*, McChrystal/Collins

30. *The 5 Dysfunctions of a Team*, Patrick M. Lencioni

31. *The 7 Hidden Reasons Employees Leave*, Leigh Branham

32. *The Five Temptations of a CEO*, Patrick M. Lencioni

33. *The Lean Start Up*, Eric Ries

34. *The One Minute Manager*, Kenneth Blanchard & Spencer Johnson

35. *The Only Way to Win*, Jim Loehr

36. *The OZ Principle*, Roger Connors

37. *The Power of Habit*, Charles Duhigg

38. *The Ultimate Question 2.0*, Fred Reichheld

39. *Think and Grow Rich*, Napoleon Hill

40. *Topgrading 3rd Edition*, Bradford D. Smart or *Who*, Geoff Smart

41. *Tribal Leadership*, Logan/King

42. *Turn the Ship Around*, David Marquet

APPENDIX

SELF ASSESSMENT

Two Options:

a. On a scale of 0 (low) to 10 (high), rate yourself on each of the following questions.

b. Optionally, you can plot your scores on a scale of 0 (low and center of the wheel) to 10 (high at the very tip of each spoke), on the Wheel of Resilience, page 107.

1. **Live an Amazing life**
    How good are you at enjoying life in tandem with your achievements in business?   _____

2. **Forget Work-Life Balance**
    Do you dedicate enough time and energy for everything that matters: your work, your self and your life?   _____

3. **Double Your Resilience**
    How good are you at making time for things that build and maintain your personal resilience: body, mind and spirit?   _____

4. **Invest in Your Sweet Spots**
    How good are you at spending the vast majority of your time and energy doing things you love, and are good at?   _____

5. **Lick Your Toads**
    How do you rate at making sure annoying little things get done before they pile up?   _____

6. **Deal with Your Emotional Junk**
    How good are you at not responding irrationally or emotionally in tense situations?   _____

7. **Manage Your Mental Health**
    How skilled are you at managing your mental health?   _____

8. **Learn Like Your Life Depends on It**
    How do you rate as a lifelong learner?   _____

9. **Get Tough Feedback**
   How do you rate at getting honest opinions about your performance?   ———

10. **Make Yourself Useless**
    How good are you at building a team so strong there's not much you need to do?   ———

11. **Quadruple Your IQ**
    How effective are you at leveraging opinions from experts, in business and in life?   ———

12. **Stop Being Chief Problem Solver**
    How skilled are you are at helping people become strong, independent leaders?   ———

13. **Teach People to Meet Your Standards**
    How skilled are you at graciously getting people to meet your high standards?   ———

14. **Tackle Tough Conversations**
    How skilled are you at quickly giving tough feedback?   ———

15. **Love the Lessons**
    How good are you at seeing the benefit in your biggest challenges, at work and in life?   ———

16. **Keep Going For It**
    How good are you at regularly stretching your personal limits?   ———

17. **Plan, Plan & Plan Again**
    How disciplined are you about planning and regularly re-planning for work, self and life?   ———

TOTALS   ———

WHEEL OF RESILIENCE

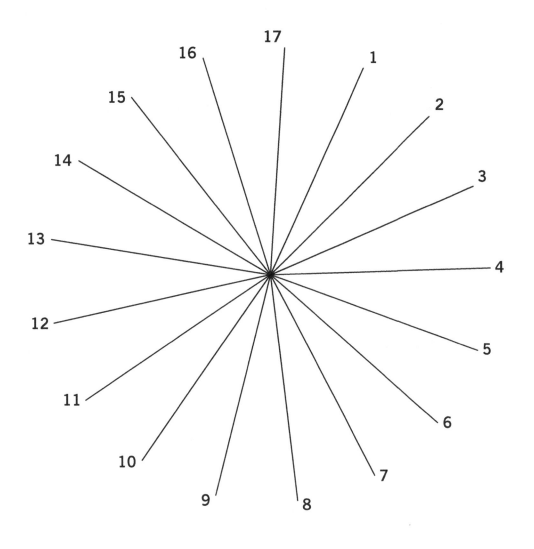

Your #1 Habit To Master: _____

_____

Why? _____

_____

About Coach Kevin

CEOs typically place their first call to Coach Kevin with a crisis to solve. They stay because of his business acumen and no-holds-barred, tell-it-like-it-is style.

Kevin's career spans 20 years and four continents. He's worked with hundreds of CEOs and executives, helping them to break through business challenges, grow their companies and find personal success along the way.

These experiences inspired Kevin's book, Your Oxygen Mask First, in which he reveals the 17 habits every leader must know to transcend the perils of success, and achieve even more.

Kevin is a Coach Emeritus with Gazelles—a rare distinction. He is a key contributor to Scaling Up (Mastering the Rockefeller Habits 2.0).

Based in Vancouver, Canada, Kevin can often be found tearing up the racetrack, or adventuring in the outdoors with his wife Angela, son Brayden and daughter Ashley.

About Lawrence & Co.

We don't do best practices. And we are not for the faint of heart.

We offer real, unvarnished insight and tools based on 20 years of actual business experience, working with some of the world's most successful high-growth companies.

We cut through fear, time-wasting and abstract theories to get our clients to sound strategies, strong balance sheets and optimal profitability.

We believe in ease and simplicity, because complexity is over-rated and inefficient.

If you want a phenomenal business and an amazing life, get in touch.

Lawrenceandco.com

Made in the USA
Middletown, DE
12 February 2020